# At the Market

by Alison Hawes

illustrated by Ley Honor Roberts

CAMBRIDGE
UNIVERSITY PRESS

UCL
Institute of Education

We go to the market to buy dinner.

I buy the fish at the market.

fish

Mum buys the spices.

spices

I buy the vegetables at the market.

vegetables

Mum buys the fruit.

fruit

I buy the rice at the market.

rice

13

Mum and I buy dinner at the market.

# At the Market  Alison Hawes

Teaching notes written by Sue Bodman and Glen Franklin

## Using this book

### Developing reading comprehension

This cumulative text shows parent and child visiting a local market to buy food for dinner. The pictures are colourful and provide lots of scope for discussion and comparison with local context. The meal at the end of the book is made from the ingredients gathered during the trip to the market.

The change in language structure on alternate pages may be challenging for children learning English as an additional language and require support by rehearsing the sentence structure orally before introducing the book.

### Grammar and sentence structure

- Support the change in language structure by attending to letter information 'buy'/'buys'.

### Word meaning and spelling

- Check vocabulary predictions by checking the first letter of the food bought at the market.
- Rehearse blending easy to hear sounds into familiar words 'go' and 'at'.
- Reinforce recognition of frequently occurring words 'the' 'to'

### Curriculum links

*Maths* – The context of buying food can link to practical mathematics activities with weight and money – *How much did each thing bought at the market cost? How much does it cost to buy vegetables and spices? Which is heavier; the fish or the rice?*

*Cookery* – Discussion of the meal could be developed into cookery activities in school or collecting favourite recipes from the cultures represented by the children.

*Language development* – Set up a shop or market play area in the classroom for the children to reinforce the language structures, vocabulary and concepts of the book in their play activities.

Other Pink B texts in this series can be used to develop one-to-one correspondence across small changes in language structure.

## Learning Outcomes

Children can:

- understand that print carries meaning and is read from left to right, top to bottom
- read some high-frequency words and use phonic knowledge to work out some simple words
- show an understanding of the sequence of events
- indicate how information can be found in non-fiction text.

## A guided reading lesson

### Book Introduction

Give a book to each child and read the title.

### Orientation

Mother and son take a trip to the market to buy ingredients for dinner. This simple expository text has one line of text on each page and using a repeated sequence of two language structures shows them visiting a range of stalls.

Give a brief orientation to the text: *Here they visit the market to buy all the things they need to make dinner. The boy buys some things and Mum buys some things.*

### Preparation

Page 2: *They go to the market. They see many different stalls and lots of different kinds of food. Let's practise pointing to every word as we read.* Make sure that everyone can match accurately as you take the lead in reading the sentence aloud.

Page 4: *Now they are going to buy something. What is boy going to buy? Yes, that's right, fish. Let's find the word 'fish' – look for the letter 'f' to help you.*

Page 6: *Now Mum is going to buy something. What does she buy? Spices? Let's check the letter – Mum buys – s is that the right letter for 'spices'? Does it make sense with the picture? Yes this is the word spices – we can check the letter and the picture.*